The Economy & My Old Troup Street Home

I decided to name this book in memory of my old Troup Street home located on south Troup Street in Valdosta, Georgia USA. I don't own the home anymore but it is still there. I lived in that old house for over twenty years.

I'm surprised that it still stands I expected that old house to be razed long ago. I wrote my first letter to the editor in that old house. I wrote the manuscript for my first book which I self-published from there.

While living there I named that old house "Villa Phoenix" and it is not even located in the countryside. Hanging from the ceiling right inside the front door was a sign that read "Welcome to Villa Phoenix."

The Lord works in mysterious ways, for awhile I had been searching and trying to think of a name to call my new book. Then one day as I was passing by that old house it dawned on me, why not honor my old home.

For some reason as I sat down to write this article and put pen to paper tears begin to flow. And to control the flood all I could do was repeat over and over to myself these words, Thank you God, Think you God, Think you God, until the storm pasted over.

1

USA NO LONGER TOTALLY IN CONTROL OF IT'S OWN DESTINY, for details read Freddie L. Sirmans, Sr. books & blogs

The founding fathers put most of the real power in the hands of the people and the states, but, the people and the states gave up their real power. The states gave up their real power by giving up the right to appoint two senate representatives every six years. And the American people give up their real power by allowing the federal government to seize and keep the family provider role for itself. Whoever carries out the family provider role are the boss and true ruler of the country.

(Scroll all the way down to read the "Devine help article")

23 NOVEMBER 2010 1527 HOURS: New update on air line search techniques.
I think the air lines, the workers, and all involved are trying their level best to make the best of a bad situation and keep the flying public safe.

Then on the other hand you have this negative constant drumbeat by much of talk radio and other arm chair quarter backs second guessing the best safety possible for the American flying public.

What this could end up doing is forcing the management into lesser security. Then guess what? Who do you think may end up taking much of the blame and heat if a plane ends up being blown out of the sky? Need I say more?

CURRENT EVENT:
22 NOVEMBER 2010, 2205 HOURS:
New comment on air line search technique.

I think a few people are trying to keep a bandwagon going. Being patted down is not new, you go back over 40 to 50 year before modern metal detecting devices and it was not uncommon at all for some night clubs to do pat downs.

Its been over 50 years when I was a young man I along with everyone else was patted down before enter a night club and no one raised any hell about it.

No court is going to touch this with a ten foot pole, because then they would be responsible for what ever happens. The people raising so much hell don't have to answer for anything if a plane is blown up.

THE AIRLINES SEARCH TECHNIQUE!

Let me get this out of the way first, having the pilots go through the same search technique is nonsense in my view.

However, folks if not the strict search technique, what is your solution? Right now the same folks pissing and moaning the loudest will be the same ones complaining the loudest if their loved ones are on a plane that blows up.

Come on folks, no one has a gun to anyone's head telling them that they gotta fly. Take your voyage by ship or other means if it's that bothersome. What are you going to tell your urologist if you have a medical problem, it is the same with the intent not to be sexual in any way?

At the rate of technology advancement today a better remedy should come about very soon. But, until that happens, I say fly safe and live because it is not about any one individual.

I seen a lady on TV get all angry and rebellious, but, she could never come up with a real or better solution, which is the case with most of the get on the bandwagon complainers.

The vast majority of the people doing that type of work dislike the technique as much as you, but these people have family to feed. And their management has a responsibility to keep everyone alive. Talk is cheap.

F L SIRMANS, SR. PLEAS FOR DIVINE

HELP!

The thing about me that make my great thinking so awesome is it is not limited in any way; it has no borders or boundaries. I have never been to economic school or taken any such classes! I don't know what is not supposed to work!

Almost all of my thinking is original; it is raw and creative from the core! Plus, my thinking takes in vastly more than the economic one leg of the whole survival stool. I'm more of a deep thinking philosopher that sees the whole survival stool and how the economy fits into the grand design.

There are infinite variables in an economy many are subjective which makes it impossible to be manage by man even with a super computer. What actually runs every economy no matter the type of government is nature's supreme law of "Natural selection."

Sure, almost any liberal bleeding heart do good economic system may work for 80-100 years, but, then the consequences of ignoring nature's supreme law of "Natural selection" catches up. And then someone is gonna pay in blood, sweat, or tears.

The nuclear and extended family system is the foundation of human survival. And is protected under nature's supreme law of "Natural selection."

So, when the welfare state for all practical purpose destroyed our nuclear and extended family system the consequences are going to make us pay dearly, hopefully we will survive as a nation.

I'm paraphrasing when I say someone complained that democracy was a terrible form of government but is still the best government known to man.

That is why I often wonder why is it so hard for nations to use an economic ideology that has never failed and have proven to always work time and time again. It will always produce an over abundance of everything.

That ideology is: "Allow free competition and let the free market place work." I think the real reason is governments just love power and the ability to control too much.

Another cold hard fact on that matter is: It is impossible to "Have free competition and a free market place" with government finger all in the pie. The more government gets involve the less of a free market place you will have.

When government sets a minimum wage which is like a vehicle with no reverse and enacts every kind or regulation and mandate one can imagine that means our USA economy doesn't even come close to being a free market place. That being the case, no one has to tell me that a total collapse is possible.

In the distance past a collapsing economy was something almost normal. It was just a rebirth or renewal. The strong nuclear and extended family system along with plenty bartering capacity would keep order until enough new growth kicked in.

We no longer have that safety valve anymore, western welfare states has just about destroyed that entire infrastructure. We no longer have a strong reliable nuclear and extended family structure anymore everybody is depending on our welfare state daddy.

Much of our moral and religious code has been reduced to what comes out of Hollywood. And we no longer have enough backup emergency bartering capacity in small farmers and home gardeners like what got us through the great depression.

This welfare state super beast has left this great nation with almost nothing in term of bare boned survival in time of crisis. We as a nation could face almost total chaos.

GOD, I ASK IN YOUR NAME, SAVE OUR GREAT NATION!
SIRMANS LOG: 9 NOVEMBER 2010, 1830

HOURS

DOOMSDAY LOG BOOK

WAL-MART CASE! Okay, if they end up socking it to Wal-mart in billions of dollars in fines who do all of those gleeful economically ignorant liberals think its really going to hurt? It certainly won't be Wal-mart in a crippling way. Who will be hurt the most is the millions of poor Americans that is struggling to keep food on the table and clothes on their kids back. All extra business cost must be passes on to the customers because if the business don't make a profit it is history.

The reason why liberals will always destroy wealth and freedom in a country is because their shallow do good intention makes them want to take all risk and failure out of life.

The shallow naive flaw in that type of thinking is human's beings is not cogs in a machine we are motivated by a complex reward or punishment response behavior. It is a law of nature that success and failure goes hand in hand and you can't have one without the other.

Just as it is as important to be able to forget things as it is to remember things but hardly anyone thinks about it that way, all of the focus is on remembering. So, when big government and the liberals prevent small purges and failures it puts the whole system at risk.

That shuts off any way to control inefficiency, crud, moral decay, and all negative anti-survival forces. Then it is only a matter of time before the negative forces of inefficiency and moral decay grow too powerful for human survival.

Also, it is impossible to create great wealth in a nation without someone willing to take a great risk and no one is going to be willing to take a great risk without individually expecting a great reward, liberals ignore this fact.

That is the reason communism and socialism will never produce wealth and riches because everyone will try to exert the least amount of energy to receive an equal reward, and that is simply human nature.

What I've said is basic kindergarten human nature knowledge; still most liberals can't comprehend these facts. A hundred years ago just day to day survival made almost everyone aware of these fact, but not since the "New deal."

It is so sad just how shallow most Americans have become since the "New deal" and our all powerful sugar daddy welfare state has become the cradle to grave great white father super provider.

Soon when this great white father super provider is broke and has a red tape death grip on all self initiative, what are we to do? God help us break this death grip and survive.

God I ask in your name give us the wisdom and strength to survive in spite of what the well intention do good liberals has unknowingly done to this great country. **SIRMANS LOG: 25 JUNE 2010, 2149 HOURS.**

UPDATED: 19 JUNE 2010, 1854 HOURS. MASS FUEL SAVING VEHICLES AIN'T GONNA HAPPEN IN THE USA!
The technology to produce a vehicle that would cut fuel consumption almost in half has been around ever since the late 1950's. From an economically point of view there are thousands of things made from oil from the pavement we drive on to the clothes on our backs, but fuel consumption is the lions share.

The reason no genuine serious effort to produce a mass fuel saving vehicle is not going to happen is because big business and the government wants more profit and revenue not less. Sure, there is some fiddling around and pretending to make a mass produced fuel saving vehicle but that is just throwing out a bone to fool the public.

If you think I'm wrong about a fuel saving vehicle take a look at the diesel locomotive. Two or three diesel locomotives can pull hundreds of box car all day long without gulping fuel. The reason is they have no drive train. The diesel engine powers a generator that supplies electrical power to electric motors for the wheels. And it's been that way ever since the late 1950's.

Sure, automobiles need quick acceleration for passing but with technology a way could be found to overcome that. All I'm saying is that in the real world what saves or works best don't always win out.

To sum it up, once the "New deal" gave the government an excuse to seize the nuclear family provider role for itself the destruction of the USA economy die was cast, estimated collapse time 4-6 generations into the future. As a super social and family provider the government is going to fight tooth and nails any and every decrease in revenue.

That is why government as a family provider will never allow a free people to remain free for very long. I have been out here screaming and hollering about the dangers of the welfare state to deaf ears now for many years.

But, I believe time is winding down and more

and more of my great wisdom is going to be realized and appreciated. I thank you God for my life, health, and strength. I carry on and refuse to stand down America.

I'm at a loss as how to think and act any other way. I give God the Praise, thank you God, thank you, thank you...

WRITERS OPINION ON STATES POWER!

I believe the main reason why the 10th amendment is totally ignored today is because of the passing of the 17th amendment. It wasn't obvious at the time but it has destroyed the balance of power between the federal government and the states.

In a real showdown the states no longer has any real power in congress because the senate is now mostly controlled by special interest. Without repealing the 17th amendment there is no stopping our welfare state beast created by liberals from both political parties.

Every day this beast is consolidating more and more power and soon states will be just designated regions. God I ask in your name, save this last bastion of true freedom in the world today, still the home of the brave, proud, and free.

ARIZONA IMMIGRATION LAW

I'm so sick and tired of hearing supposedly intelligent people believing that this or that official hasn't read the Arizona immigration law. My God! That is one of the oldest lawyer tricks in the book.

One of the hardest things there is is to get a lawyer to admit having read anything unless it is in his/her best interest. Of course, they all have read the Arizona immigration law, but you can't prove it and question someone on something they don't know anything about. Case closed.

IMMIGRATION HYPOCRITES GALORE!
I'm going to give you the cold steel or rock hard facts on immigration because no one else is going to say it out loud. The first fact is it will be impossible to solve the immigration symptom and I say symptom because the welfare state is the root problem.

All I hear is a lot of hypocritical nonsense on the subject and no one wanting to face cold hard facts. The USA can't feed itself or survive if it had to depend only on Americans to do field work and many other hard labor jobs.

Sure, I hear a lot of talk to the otherwise that is cheap, but try to tell a farmer with his harvest rotting in the field that kind of nonsense. You may not agree with me but I'll tell you how to solve the immigration problem, kick the welfare state the hell out of its super sugar daddy social and family provider role. And send it back to its designated role of collecting taxes, and protecting and defending the country.

As long as we have our existing welfare state it is futile and a waste of time and grandstanding for any politician to talk about solving the immigration symptom.

Far too many able bodied men in America don't have to work and especially doing hard labor, they can always sponge off of a mother, sister, aunt, or grandmother that is on the dole. For God sake, give me a break America.

President Ronald Wilson Reagan only had to deal with 3 millions illegals and here we are around 30 years later and around 30 millions illegals and guess what, many of the same people are still around singing the same old cop-out blues.

For God sake, give these people season work permits so they can come and go as they please and stop being hypocrites and face reality. They won't go home now because they are afraid they can't come back and work, a work permit is the only sensible thing to do.

Otherwise, they won't go home and in a few

years we'll have 50 million and the same old song will still be playing and nothing will have changed as long as this welfare state has any say.

Europe doesn't have the illegal immigration problem like in the USA. The reason is they use a common sense approach like a guest worker permit.

However, something so simple and reasonable will never happen in the USA because the liberals are more interesting in gaining new voters to keep them in power than solving the problem.

WRITERS OPINION ON PUTTING ETHANOL IN GASOLINE!

I think putting ethanol in gasoline was one of the cruelest hoaxes ever pulled on the American people. Anyone that have an older or any car that is seldom driven is going to have problems.

With ethanol in it gasoline deteriorates so rapid that the gas tank needs draining after a month or so if not used. Plus, sooner or later it is going to drive the cost of all corn products out of sight.

I have an old classic car that I seldom drive and I gotta find me some ethanol free gasoline somewhere. Sometime later, shame on you Freddie Sirmans Sr, for thinking there is still individual freedom left in the USA to buy ethanol free gasoline!

Hell, how was I to know that it is mandated by the Feds that ethanol free gasoline can no longer be found in this great free country. I guess I will just have to drain all of the gas out of my old classic car and keep the tank empty or run the hell out of it. Wakeup America!

SIRMANS LOG: 12 MAY 2010, 0029 HOURS.

I have been wrong before and may be wrong on this. I just can't bring myself to believe that the liberals will actually vote anyone on to the United States Supreme Court that don't have a long established liberal ruling record.

In my mind it just doesn't add up, so I'm going to call the bluff and up the ante. I think they want to soften up the opposition before sending in a die hard liberal with a long established liberal ruling record.

Remember folks, I'm just thinking out loud here I have no reason to think this except a gut feeling of my own. I just don't trust liberals with power. We'll see, Maybe they know something the rest of us don't that will trump a long proven liberal ruling record.

However, my gut feeling is they don't and a

stalking horse strategy is being used. There is no doubt about it, it is the roll of the dice on the part of the liberals, who really knows they probably hit the jackpot, but only history will give us the proof with a proven liberal ruling record.

SIRMANS LOG: 10 MAY 2010, 1444 HOURS.

WRITER STRESSES A POINT: 8 MAY 2010, 1453 HOURS.

These guys on TV were talking about spending and one made the point that government spending money comes from businesses and the taxpayers.

I agree, but, that is not the whole truth and nothing but the truth. You want the real truth! I'll give it to you! All government income originates from some form of business profit.

"Profit" and nothing but profit can create wealth. When you tax choke to death the goose that lays the golden egg you go to the poor house or you starve. However, you can never get a liberal to understand that simple fact.

The problem with economics is not enough Americans understand it not even trained economist. The first rule is you can't separate the economy from culture and human behavior.

The next thing is using money is supposed to be only an easier means of trading and bartering, societies survived with trading and bartering long before money or a currency was invented.

Actually, the value of money is supposed to be in the money itself in the form of gold, silver, or some other precious metal, not some worthless paper backed only on faith.

It started when someone suggested why carry around all of this heavy money why not let the government print a paper note and lock the gold and silver away as a backup.

That worked just fine until the "New deal" came along and opened the door for the government to seize the traditional family provider role for itself.

Once government got a taste of the God like power of being a super sugar daddy provider the politicians went hog wild and is still spending like there is no tomorrow.

The gold backup did survive until President Richard M. Nixon just flat outright outlawed it, then the liberals from both political parties with little or no resistance found themselves in spending hog heaven and are still having a field day.

Life itself is a process of cycles and rebirths, success and failure are part of our existence and there is absolutely nothing man can do to change that fact.

That means booms, busts, good times, hard times, famines, and horrible acts of nature are always going to come around sooner or later. The only tried and true protection that has allowed man and civilization to survive over the years is to maintain and safeguard a strong culture.

A strong culture must have a strong nuclear and extended family system, a strong religious or moral code in place, and adequate backup bartering capacity, we have very little of that left.

A physical valued or gold backed currency will safe guard a nations culture by purging or holding at bay the negative anti-survival forces like moral decay, left and right extremes, and porn.

Now, the only way to save the USA is to some how rebuild her culture, but that can never happen unless the people and the states vote the welfare state beast out of its super provider role.

I knew when the liberals finally got the elderly on government health care it was going to be almost impossible to save individual freedom and America itself. Once you make people your dependents very few are going to bite the hand that feeds them.

Now, nearly 50 percent of the American people are heavily government dependent and don't pay any federal income taxes, how can you expect people to vote against their own self interest, you can't.

The nation is on a suicide mission with little or no hope of individual freedom surviving, and even worse the young and average American still don't get it, especially the mostly liberal news media. Please God, help me educate this great nation.

This is a stress call for our survival as a free people. The big plus with getting back to a real physical currency with the value self contained within itself is it would assure survival of the people no matter how stupid the government acted.

The currency would be protected against all inflation and if you buried it or hid it under the mattress it would keep its value. Also, it would put most of the financial power back into the hands of the people.

I don't see any way USA sovereignty can be saved with the financial course we are on, the UN. or some world body will end up owning us if we don't get back to a real currency.

However, getting back to a real currency is something the people will have to demand because politicians and the government will never give up wielding their super provider God like power.

They will stop at nothing to continue trying to do the impossible which is to keep our welfare state beast fed. There is not enough money in the whole wide world to keep financing our welfare state, but the liberals are in complete denial and are taking the great USA down for the count.

Even today if you found a buried treasure hidden by a black beard over 600 years ago its value would be just as much because the value and worth is self-container within the precious metal itself.

WRITER SHARES SOME PERSONAL EXPERIENCE!

Freedom is something the average American takes for granted. While we sleep comfortable in our cozy warm beds at night very few of us ever take time to think that vigilantly standing guard every second twenty four hours everyday protecting us is our military.

It's been a long time now nearly fifty years ago when I was active duty military and played my small part physical and up close. I have seen up close some of the might that protects us.

The old Atlas ICBM's have long been retired now, but I have been down five floors deep into the bowels of a missile silo in the Nebraska countryside as a young U.S. Air Force firefighter.

Someone said something to this effect, "Freedom is never free."

God, I ask in your name save our great country.
SIRMANS' LOG: 18 APRIL 2010, 0944 HOURS.

The thing about a 3rd party vote is there is no consolation prize it is an all of nothing game, and 99.9 percent of the time nothing is what one gets.

Everybody knows that a 3rd party movement only guarantees victory to the opposing major party, that is a given, there is no getting around that fact.

So, I say concede failure possibilities, go for broke, damn the torpedoes' full steam ahead, put it all on the line, sink or swim, it ain't over til the fat lady sings, never say never, No guts no glory is my advice to a 3rd party.

To hell with being hemmed in look what it has gotten freedom loving Americans. We have two main political parties in the USA and the only major difference is speed. One party is rushing into full socialism at warp speed and the other is crawling with a drip, drip slow motion torture into full socialism.

Sure, the liberals with their nearly 50 percent hardcore government dependents are going to win for now. But, I'm going to stake all of my God given wisdom on the fact that the American people will never accept a political system that brings undue hardship, starving, and suffering.

Individual freedom is bred into the American people and I don't believe they are going to tolerate a system like in Europe. Socialism never has and never will work it only gets worse with time.

If a 3rd party make a stand the people will come to them when they see socialism up close. That will especially be true if the two major parties keep growing government. **SIRMANS' LOG: 15 APRIL 2010, 1129 HOURS.**

Since I have been giving my strong opinion on a lot of things lately I decided to go whole hog all the way and make it a clean slate. Hell, it could be the smoking gun to some and finally confirm that I really am off my rocker.

I didn't have to do this; I could have forever

kept this a deep dark secret and took it with me to my grave. Well, here goes my true belief on what I am about to admit to the whole wide world.

I would say I do believe to the tune of about 99.9 percent but I just can't bring myself to make it a complete 100 percent. "I don't believe that man has ever set foot on the moon."

Sure, I know the USA has orbited the moon with astronauts and broadcasted about landing and taking off from the moon. But, I believe the pictures were taken in the Nevada desert or somewhere like that. So, how do you like me now?

SIRMANS' LOG: 8 APRIL 2010, 1659 HOURS.

NEW TRAIL BLAZING BREAKTHROUGH WEIGHT LOSING BATTLE!
A word of advice about changing eating behavior, it can be done but it is not a simple or easy matter. The only guarantee is to never stop repeating the quote because fat cells don't like being starved. One may start craving sweets and wanting to eat everything in sight and feeling the quote is a waste of time all to get you to quit repeating the quote.

(Scroll down to bottom for latest weight losing battle progress report entry.)

Anyone familiar with my writing knows that I have a super strong belief in "positive thinking" to change behavior. To those that don't know what positive thinking is, I will explain.

It is a technique to change behavior; take a phrase or quote and repeats it over and over to yourself. It doesn't need to be repeated aloud.

However, to be effective it must be repeated at least fifty or more times every day. The more times it is repeated the faster it will work because it is the repeating process itself that breaks through to the subconscious.

The quote to repeat is: I can keep small all of my food portions, (through God which strengthens me)." The through God part can be left out or changed to fit ones own deity if desired. It may take as long as a year or longer to fully kick in, and bear fruit, but if one doesn't quit the repeating process is guaranteed to get results.

Just keep repeating the quote to yourself at least 50 times or more every day, and never quit until your goal is reached. God will make a way out of no way. Mighty forces will come to your aid. It will work if one doesn't quit.

A word of advice about changing eating

behavior, it can be done but it is not a simple or easy matter. The only guarantee is to never stop repeating the quote because fat cells don't like being starved. One may start craving sweets and wanting to eat everything in sight and feeling the quote is a waste of time all to get you to quit repeating the quote.

The body cells in cahoots with the mind will play all kinds of tricks to get you to quit but in the end you will reach your goal if you stay with it and never quit. It is like breaking in a wild horse.

The wild horse is going to buck and try everything in its power to throw you off but if you can hang on and ride it out you will obtain your goal. The reason it is so hard to lose weight is your body cells in cahoots with your mind will use reward and punishment against you.

The punishment of hunger may seem much more severe. And at the same time the good taste of food may seem much more rewarding. However, in the end the mind must try to carry out any image constantly presented to it.

WEIGHT BATTLE BEGINS!
I, Freddie L. Sirmans, Sr. have decided to share with my readers the inner working of my mind out loud as I try to discover

secrets on how to lose weight.

The tactics I try may not work; still, I decided to share with my readers as I plot my strategy on defeating my sometimes overpowering compulsive overeating habit.

WARNING: I check with my doctor before trying anything new or stressful.

The previous positive thinking quote with enough time is effective, but, I've decided to create this newer untested quote developed by me anyway. I don't fully recommend it yet because it may cause some stress. And anyone that uses it does it at their own risk.

Positive thinking has been proven to change behavior when the same quote or phrase is repeated to oneself at least 50 times or more every day. The more times it is repeated the faster it works. The quote to repeat, which I don't recommend yet is to just say over and over: **"Eating too much food is dangerous."**

Positive thinking is a slow process, sometimes it can take 6 months to a year or even longer to fully kick in.

Just as our main survival responses are fight or flight, reward or punishment are the main responses that control our behavior. Nothing in nature is all good or all bad; it is a matter of degree and balance.

The reward of pleasure and good taste is necessary to make sure we eat, but, the balance arm of too much is not kicking in with compulsive over eaters like me.

So, maybe through "Positive thinking" an artificial overriding braking system will work. There is nothing to lose but weight.

The problem of overeating starts from eating when not hungry for whatever reason. Once the "Don't eat when not hungry" response is shoved completely out of the picture, for some, overeating becomes a compulsion.

Then any attempt to limit the amount and push away from the table is looked upon as a cruel punishment and taking away a deserved reward.

The key is to realize that too much food intake is really a punishment of survival instead of just a harmless too much of a good thing reward.
10 NOVEMBER 2010, 1853 HOURS: Last entry.

19 NOVEMBER 2010, 1708 HOURS: New Progress report
in my quest to discover secrets on losing weight I will use the "Positive thinking"

technique on myself to gauge my progress.

From my previous entry I established that it is reward or punishment that controls all normal human behavior. Also, I established that once the "Don't eat when not hungry" response is ignored enough the inner mind then see all eating including over eating as a reward. Then no amount of eating is viewed as punishment and stomach capacity becomes the only stopping point.

Now, the first strategy I'm going to use is to set eating rules followed by punishment for every infraction of those rules.

Rule number one: I'm going to decide on what weight I plan to get down to and list it on paper. My current weight is 252LBS and my goal weight is 195LBS.

Rule number two: I'm going to limit all meals to one helping, no second for anything.

Rule number three: Set everything I plan to eat before me before I start, after that no going back for seconds. Once I start eating and notice something I really like and want, I'll just remember I can have it my next meal 4 hours later.

Rule number four: No snacking between meals.

Rule number five: No meals will be eaten at less than four hour intervals. All rules and conditions may be waived if I'm sick or doing extra strenuous work.

Rule number six: Unlimited amounts of water are permitted at all times, but Juices, sodas, or high protein drinks are permitted only at four hours intervals

Snacking is something that needs to be discouraged. Contrary to what people think most people are not overweight because of extra large over powering meals, but because of snacking on junk foods and sweets, especially kids.

Remember reward or punishment is what shapes all behavior and that includes eating behavior. So, that means if I break one of my own eating rules I must punish myself for the infraction.

Whoa, hold on, I'm not talking about any harsh, cruel, or diabolical like punishment, but still, a message must be sent that rule breaking will not be tolerated.

The punishment stick I'm going to use on myself is going to be the punishment of fasting limited to juices, sodas, high protein drinks, or water but absolutely no food.

All punishment will be limited to a minimum

of 4 hours up to a maximum of 24 hours. I'm going to assign a set punishment for certain infractions for now and may add more later.

SET PUNISHMENTS:
(1.) Punishment for all rules except snacking: 12 hours of fasting limited to juices, sodas, or high protein drinks at not less than 4 hour intervals. I can drink water anytime, but absolutely no food for 12 hours.

(2.) Punishment for breaking the "No snacking" rule: 4 hours of fasting limited to water only but absolutely no food.

Here is the skinny on the rule violations that is something I must enforce or else abandon this whole thing right now. That is because I have challenged my inner mind for dominance over my compulsive over eating habits and if I don't follow through with enforcement, my inner mind will come roaring back with a vengeance.

I may start craving sweet and wanting to eat everything in sight and end up gaining weight and eating more than ever. That is why any serious major change in behavior is always going to cause some temporary stress.

I've decided to start repeating my latest **"Eating too much food is dangerous"** positive thinking quote. Also, you keep checking I plan to make at least monthly progress reports.

19 NOVEMBER 2010, 2130 HOURS: Last entry
21 NOVEMBER 2010, 2025 HOURS: New progress report.
To more consolidate my new dominance over my compulsive over eating disorder I have started a 24 hour fasting tactic. I will be doing a 24 hour fast every week until I reach my weight goal of 195LBS.

The fast will start every Sunday at 12 o'clock noon and end the next day 12 o'clock noon on Monday. Unlimited amounts of water are permitted at all times but juices, sodas, or high protein drinks are permitted only at four hour intervals.

There is no restriction on the amount of juices, sodas, or high protein drinks consumed at a setting. Also, there is no set amount of meals per day, but no meal is permitted to be served less than a 4 hour interval.

WEIGHT PROGRESS REPORT:
MONTH---YEAR--STARTED Wt.----CURRENT WT.
November 2010---252Lbs----------250LBS
December 2010--------------------247LBS
January 2011--------------------
February 2011-------------------
March 2011----------------------

April 2011------------------------
May 2011-------------------------
June 2011-----------------------
July 2011------------------------
August 2011----------------------
September 2011------------------
October 2011---------------------
November 2011-------------------
December 2011-------------------

21 NOVEMBER 2010, 1045 HOURS: Last entry.

LESS STRESS MORE SUCCESS WITH THIS PRAYER

To my father who is in heaven I will strive to always serve you first. I will strive to treat all people well as I would like to be treated. I will strive to wish all people goodwill even when it is not returned. I will strive to repeat this prayer twice a day for as long as I live. I thank you God for my life health and strength and for what I do have here on earth. I can face and do all things through you my God. Amen.

A PRAYER GUARANTEED FOR LESS STRESS AND MORE SUCCESS!!!

To my father who is in heaven I will strive to always serve you first. I will strive to treat all people well as I would like to be treated. I will strive to wish all people goodwill even when it is not returned. I will strive to repeat this prayer twice a day for as long as I live. I thank you God for my life health and strength and for what I do have here on earth. I can face and do all things through you my God. Amen.

This prayer was created by self-made writer Freddie L. Sirmans, Sr. mainly to aid the African American people but it is for anyone that finds it useful. Because of so much violent infighting within the African American community he felt the need to create this prayer.

Mr. Sirmans knows this prayer works and in six months will rid much of the negative thinking and myth's that holds so many back and keeps them down.

Proof of a pudding is in the taste, proof of this prayer is your stress level and positive outlook after saying it a while. This prayer is not limited to just my own belief one can make a substitution and use their own deity.
.

I will guarantee you that anyone who says this prayer twice a day for 6 months will be healed or ninety percent improved. It won't matter if its stress or any other condition a new positive outlook and change will take place. However, you will never find out if you don't test it for yourself.

POST STATEMENT (PS :) I, Freddie L.

Sirmans, Sr. gives my direct permission to whom ever it may concern that he/she can copy this prayer and promote it anyway he/she see fit providing not a single word is changed.

Signed: Freddie L. Sirmans on this 14th day of February two thousand ten (2010).

GREAT HEALING QUOTES

In childhood when a child is under grave mental or physical threats and abuse the mind will go to extreme lengths to instill emotional images to assure survival under adverse conditions. Another example: We all have heard the term "Animal magnetism or something chemical." Well, in my view, super powerful emotional sexual energy like that comes from some form of childhood sexual abuse.

As a young child being punished as a bed wetter caused me to have neurotic symptoms for as long as I can remember. Today I'm over sixty seven years of age and for the last forty years I've used positive thinking as a tool to try to solve the riddle of my neurotic symptoms. And after all of these years I've come to one conclusion, you can't solve the riddle, but, you can face it down. Another thing I've learned is the real hidden enemy is "un-forgiveness."

It makes some turn on themselves and self-destruct. It makes some turn on others and cause great destruction to others. My offer of help to others battling and struggling with this hidden enemy is: There is hope and relief if you are willing to learn forgiveness. Not everyone wants to learn forgiveness. I feel blessed and thankful that all of my effort over the years has not been wasted.

I have developed more than one positive thinking quote over the years, but I believe this one is my "Holy Grail." As always, the positive thinking technique is to take a quote and repeat it to yourself over and over at a minimum of fifty times a day. It helps to repeat it more because the more it is repeated the faster it works. It is not enough to believe and know it works; the repeating process itself is what breaks through to the subconscious.

My life long guaranteed Holy Grail positive thinking quote is: "I can face and forgive all things,"(optional) through God who strengthens me.

CONCERNING TOURETTE SYNDROME AND OTHER PHOBIA'S:

I saw a program on TV the other day on Tourette syndrome and it made me think that disease over in my mind. The first thing in my view is instead of people taking all of these mind altering drug with side effects, I believe my "Holy grail" positive thinking quote offers a superior natural remedy. The working of the mind deals only in images and it doesn't distinguish between a good image and a bad image; it just obeys the strongest command image presented.

The reason may be an unloving environment or any threat to ones survival that causes an emotion to stamp a survival image on ones mind against the will of a weaken ego. The natural reaction of the ego is to resist any unacceptable image, which can be counterproductive, because that is what stamps the unwanted image on the subconscious mind. Therefore, the harder one tries to mentally resist any emotional image the more strongly the image becomes and the mind will obey the strongest command image.

Example:
The more one fears he is going to do or say something shocking the more likely that fear will over power his ego and make it happen.
Decoded:
Fear actually means lack of emotional resistance energy and the more one fears he is going to lose, the harder the mind tries to obey the command image to lose. That is why animals can smell fear and go in for an easy kill. Remember, the emotions are super powerful images, but they can never defeat the ego if the ego calls their bluff. No emotion can force the ego to do anything that it really doesn't want to do.

In childhood when a child is under grave mental or physical threats and abuse the mind will go to extreme lengths to instill emotional images to assure survival under adverse conditions. Another example: We all have heard the term "Animal magnetism or something chemical." Well, in my view, super powerful emotional sexual energy like that comes from some form of childhood sexual abuse.

I haven't studied psychology or anything of the sort, but I have enough common sense to know that things like sexual obsession and sexual projections have to do with childhood sexual abuse. Just count yourself lucky if you have never had to escape from someone abused and cursed with this energy. Once involved for some reason it is extremely hard to get someone like that out of your mind because of their primitive enticing sexual power.

They have the ability to turn one on to a super sexual charged level. Also, most people cursed with this energy tend to be abusers themselves. Because of the power of the mind a molester may start off being in control, but the table can get flipped on him, that is why some accuse their victim of being possessed.

So, when you see a previously well controlled

individual completely fall apart in a new relationship, don't be so quick to condemn. There are energy forces out there that only a super strong moral person can resist. When these victims are back in a normal environment without any threats those same powerful emotional images may still be protecting them the same way making them seem weird and abnormal in close contact.

Now, my solution is to deal with the situation in a tandem way. Like I said, the emotions have no real power, except to bluff and put up a facade. So, when confronted by overpowering self-guilt and self-shame all one has to do is call their bluff by facing them head on and in short order they will start fading away, that makes "Facing" the keyword. Now, to the other side of the tandem. To instill a strong healthy ego in a child it is so important for that child to have at least some love and acceptance.

Otherwise, the emotions of fear, shame, and guilt can leave the child vulnerable to all sorts of mental illnesses. There is a world of difference between being the way one wants to be and being the way one really is. So, if one has self images he can't accept for whatever reason, no amount of wishful thinking is going to change that fact. When the ego hates the way one is, the emotions of self-shame and self-guilt can make one feel worthless and unworthy.

Self-shame, self-guilt, and self-hate can destroy the mental self (ego) the same as if someone physical blows one's brains out. In this case, "Forgiveness" is the keyword. Therefore, my positive thinking natural remedy is: "I can face and forgive all things (optional) through God who strengthens me." "I can face and forgive all things." "I can face and forgive all things......

Forgiveness
1. It is the only thing that will ease embedded anger and hate.
2. If one has been hurt and mistreated, especially by a friend or loved one, forgiveness may be the only thing that will ease ones raging anger and desire to reject, avenge, destruct, or destroy.
3. There are no greater powers on earth than love and forgiveness.
4. There is no mental condition or problem that love and forgiveness can't heal.
5. Nothing can mental defeat one that can genuine love and forgive.
6. You can't change other people but other people will respond to a change in you.
7. it's a proven fact that the power of positive thinking can change behavior.
8. To acquire genuine joy and happiness it is one of the best tools, but only the truly unselfish will forgive no matter how they are treated in return.
9. To acquire this awesome power, repeat to

yourself fifty or more times a day the following "world's most powerful healing quote" whenever and as long as necessary.

10. THE WORLD'S MOST POWERFUL HEALING QUOTE IS:

"I can wish all people goodwill no matter how they treat me." Note: To be effective one should never repeat more than one quote at a time during a six month period.

11. Actually wishing all people goodwill even if its not returned is not to please others, but to mentally and emotionally guarantee a bright future for yourself. It is still true that "Attitude determine altitude." You are how you treat all people including those you have power over when no one else is around. So, if you remain a loving, caring, and forgiving person you will reap those rewards in life.

Note:

Forgiveness does not mean that one tolerates abuse or mistreatment in any way. You separate yourself from any abusive situation, then forgive and move on. As a rule the choices we make determines our fate. But, self preservation should always come first.

MR. SIRMANS VIEW ON CHRISTIANITY:

Mr. Sirmans for one doesn't believe modern civilization would be where it is today without Christianity. He thinks the main ingredient in Christianity that allows it to advance civilization more than any other religion is its emphasis on forgiveness, and the "Sermon on the mount" message.

It may not seem like much, but without the power of forgiveness, foreign and domestically everyone could still be emphasizing tit for tat, eye for eye, tooth for tooth, regressing back to the Stone Age. That is what some countries would do if left entirely to themselves. Lastly, I must include a count your bless quote as a stress reliever because of so many people on legal mind altering drugs.

True joy and happiness is determine by how one accepts and appreciate life, not what one have or may not have. The old biblical advice is still true today as it was five thousand years ago. Remember to count your blessings, or never forget to count your blessings. As always the power in positive thinking is in the repeating process itself. Whenever one is feeling down and stressed out, repeat this quote over and over to yourself, "Thank you God for my life, health, and strength, thank you, thank you....

Another good positive quote to repeat to yourself when you just can't seem to make ends meet is, " Thank you God for what I do have, Thank you, thank you...Say it as much and as long as necessary until the storm passes over. This is from the horse's mouth itself. Over the years I've used this quote to get over my darkest hours. There have been times when I've felt totally unlovable with no hope to ever find happiness.

All I knew to do was put one foot in front of the other and go through the motion of living. But, deep down in my soul there was always an unwavering fighting instinct to survive. So far back I can't even remember I instinct knew that if one can refuse to hate he cannot be mentally destroyed. I knew that as long as one can genuine love and forgive someway somehow he would triumph in the end.

You will never see those that can genuine love and forgive in mental wards and stressed out loser with no hope. Enough said, thank you for taking the time to read my work.

STARVING IS THE DEADLIEST THREAT TO THE UNITED STATES!

When I say a hundred million could starve to death there is a reason. Never in history before the welfare state has any nation been without a strong nuclear family system, a strong religious and moral code, and plenty of small farmers and home gardeners with fallback bartering capacity. We are in no man land, never has any nation dealt with a situation with no means to hold a society together, we are facing total chaos with survival of only the strongest and fittest.

There are many people that wonder what

make Freddie L. Sirmans, Sr. tick? Well, I'm
not so sure myself and I know me better than
anyone. Personality-wise, I being a writer am
almost like a fish out of water. I may not
show it but deep down I can be secretive,
suspicious minded, and reclusive to a fault.
All of that said, I still decided to share some
of my inner thoughts and beliefs.

There is one thing I never want and have
waged an internal battle and struggle against
all of my life that is self-pity. No one can truly
know what goes on in the mind of another
human being. The self-pity thing! The first
neurotic symptom I experienced as a very
young child was a physical look of self-pity for
being physical punished for wetting the bed. I
believe the end product of any adult is mostly
what comes out of childhood.

It's not talked about, but the human mind will
go to extreme lengths to aid in ones survival,
especially the very young. The neurotic self-
pity look was my minds way of trying to
assure my survival. The mind can give an
abused child super natural sexual powers of
projection, which may cause all kinds of
unintended consequences. Even when one
has great genes I believe the environment is
still by far the biggest factor in how one turns
out.

Whoa! Don't be so quick to judge, the lord
works in mysterious ways. I truly think God

for the way I am, or what I do have. The hardest thing is to learn to love and forgive something you hate and something's you shouldn't, but things about yourself you should. Self-shame, self-guilt, self-pity, etc. are emotions that can completely disable any human being. Many things that most people take for granted are cut off to me.

Sure, I could spend a lifetime learning to do things now cut off to me, but I feel when destiny reaches out and selects you for a mission it is because of who you are, not who you want to be.

I never set out to be a writer, I just got tired of being mistreated, and felt at least somebody would know Freddie L. Sirmans, Sr. deserves some respect. There has been no stone unturned looking into my life. There! I've said it! I have bared part my soul! How much will it cost me?

Look at history! In any profession when an original thinker like me speaks reality and common sense professional ideologues has always closed their eyes and ears. Look at the closed minds Sister Kenny (nurse) faced in trying to aid polio victims. The buggy whip industry had a closed mind against the automobile. And the automobile industry had a closed mind against leaving any trolley car tracks in place anywhere in the country.

However, reality can be put off only so long, then it will start settling in whether one likes it or not. The rock hard cold reality is, "The galloping cost of living and the dwindling buying power of the dollar" is what's killing our economy. No amount of bail outs or stimulus packages is going to save us because that is barking up the wrong tree. Anyone reading enough of my writing soon realizes that it must be super natural inspired or the ranting of a lunatic. You decide!

STARVING IS THE DEADLIEST THREAT TO THE UNITED STATES!

Food is the number one priority for survival. In the end food is going to be the real undoing of this welfare state. None of the other lesser priorities such as culture, bartering, currency (money), or even the lack of oil are the deadliest threats to this nation. The deadliest threat to this nation is a hundred million or more people starving to death when the economy collapses.

And anybody that thinks it can't happen is a Damn fool. We have almost no bartering capacity. And a strong nuclear family system is almost nonexistent. Those are the two primary things that have allowed civilization to exist for over five thousand years.

Our morals and values are so corrupted that when the going gets rough millions of people are going to have to die un-necessarily just to maintain order. The masses of welfare state dependents have no true sense of self-discipline or self-initiative, they think the federal government is omnipotent. The welfare state is what killed off this nation's small farmer and home gardeners, they was this nation's emergency breadbasket.

They furnished this nation with a huge bartering capacity and would have been the backup to sustain this nation during a financial collapse or nuclear crisis. They got this nation through the great depression. Our current welfare state has left us with almost no bartering capacity or hardly any means of surviving if the government does go belly-up.

A nation with no bartering capacity is like having a dagger aimed at its heart in terms of long term survival. Sure, the huge centralized mechanized factory farms are feeding us now, but provide almost no national bartering capacity. They are extremely dependent on mass quantities of fuel made from oil, and they are hundreds of miles away.

That means if there are bottle necks or fuel problems, millions of mouths could go without food. As it is now this nation could be in grave danger even with a small national crisis that last over three days. People could start hoarding and bottle necks could pop up everywhere. Yet, I'm seen as a nut case for wanting to be prepared to survival under all conditions.

Big liberal media knows who I am, because I've been out here beating the bushes for a lot of years, now (no pun intended). The good thing about beating the bushes is, if nothing else, it eventually drives the political snakes out into the open.

With modern political polling almost every politician is just pandering to what he thinks the people want to hear. So, a word of warning is be careful what you wish for, you just might get it, but in sheep clothing. I have personally seen opportunist people change from like night to day with just a small taste of money or power.

Freddie L. Sirmans' lecture on understanding an economy.
The fact is very few people today actually understand how an economy is supposed to works, even some learned economist. The minute the government took on a free cash give-out provider role the US destruction die was cast. Under current conditions it is now impossible to control inflation. I feel it necessary to give a brief lecture in my opinion on how an economy works.

John produces enough food for his family and him to eat plus a little extra to sell for a profit. But John can only produce a small amount for profit. So, to make more profit

John needs a helper, but he must share the extra profit with the helper in the form of a salary. He is now a proprietor and can continue to expand as long as his profit margin will allow it. The keyword is profit, profit, profit, and more profit.

To all of these liberals that think jobs just drop out of heaven and big business is the boogie man, try living without profit. An economy actually consists of only two players no matter how advanced and complicated it becomes, a seller and a buyer. Anyone else involved is just crashing the party. Let's use merchant as the seller and consumer as the buyer.

This evil boogie man that's called "Inflation" can never take over a true natural economy. That is because the merchants can never charge more than the poorer consumers can afford and stay in business. From necessity a third player must enters the economy picture for security reasons, that player is the government.

Government itself is not part of a functional economy. It is a necessary parasite that is needed to protect the economy and society. Government is not a threat to an economy as long as it takes its cut off the top and fulfills its role as a protector. The trouble starts when government takes its tax revenue cut and starts interfering in the economical process itself thereby disrupting the natural balance between the merchant and the consumer.

There are only two players, the merchant and the consumer in an economy. So, when government uses its take to subsidize the poorer group of consumers on an individual basis, it allows the merchants to survive their price raise for everyone and ignite inflation on everyone.

The balance arm is a strong nuclear family. Throughout history before the welfare state a merchant could never raise prices above what the poor could afford to pay because the poor could turn to the nuclear family for support. Plus, there were many small farmers and home gardeners and never enough rich and well-to-do to support the merchant's too high prices.

There must be a government to protect a society from internal and external threats. The thing about government is it has the power and the guns. So, dictator and authoritarian type governments take over and runs the whole show. Nothing has changed, authoritarian type governments have never been able feed themselves.

Throughout distance history they would conquer other countries and make them slaves or work almost for nothing. Only free people with a free market place will produce enough for everyone to eat. Otherwise, one will do just enough to keep from getting shot.

There is no problem or threat to an economy with government in the picture. And having government in the picture will not activate inflation if it avoids handing out money on an individual basis. Government spending itself doesn't activate inflation; it's how it does the spending.

Government can spend like crazy and build hospitals, bridges, roads, or whatever and it won't activate inflation because that doesn't affect the relationship between the merchants and the consumers. The government can give the poor food, clothing, housing or whatever and it still won't activate inflation. But, the one thing the government should never do because it will wake up and unleash the sleeping monster called "Inflation."

That one thing is the government giving out free cash money to the poor or anyone else on an individual basis. The "Individual basis" is the deadly time bomb fuse. What that does is disrupt the natural selection process between the merchant and the consumer and activates a never ending inflationary spiraling monster. How this work is there are never enough rich people to keep overly high cost merchants in business.

So, the government with good intentions gives the poor enough free cash money to afford the merchant's high price. In the beginning that made all parties happy. Then the government raised taxes to give out more cash so the poor could support even higher merchant prices, and upped the ante even higher by throwing in food stamps and countless social programs.

The merchants called, and again raised their prices. And again the government called, then raised taxes even higher, and around and around it goes in this never ending inflationary spiral. That is what got us to where we are today.

Trading and bartering have been around as long as civilization itself. A true free market place will always produce enough food to feed everyone at an affordable price if allowed to. All that is necessary is for the government to get the hell out of the way, and stick to its true role as administrator and protector of society. That means collect the taxes its due, and the economy will take care of its self with government out of the way.

It won't be pretty but if allowed to the natural selection process and entrepreneurs will feed the poor and everyone at an affordable price. However, that will never take place when dictators and over controlling governments choke off self-initiative, self-greed, and self-interest. The above are the most powerful energy packed motivating forces in our human makeup. Sure, you must control these forces but never completely choke them off if you want a rich and powerful society.

Some may ask, what about all of these people depending on the government. In my view the government caused the problem and is responsible for providing whatever is necessary for these people to survive. But, we must get off this ever increasing merry-go-round inflationary spiral before inflation eats up the last crumb of any dollar buying power.

Almost everyone thinks without government help the poor can't make it, but in reality it was just the opposite before the welfare state destroyed everything. There are over five thousand years of history that backs me up on this. Sure, the poor will always need help from somewhere, but it should come from the nuclear family, the extended family, the church, and community organizations.

Human survival is based on need involving a natural selection process. When the government with its power becomes a sugar daddy provider it takes away the survival need for the strong nuclear family, extended family, etc. Now, if the economy collapses the government can't provide for its dependents and other debts and burdens, and all I can say is "Lord helps us."

Even the people that remember the "The Hoover days" with the struggles during the "Great depression" never had their spirits dampened like they are today. I will not break my pen, I will never stop trying to sound the alarm as long as there is breath in me, and this welfare state is slowly skinning this nation alive. I want my grand children to be free.

In my view when it comes to forms of government, nothing is more deadly for destruction than a welfare state, not even communism or socialism. The welfare state is a new monster that only came about within the last fifty years since money no longer has value in itself or a gold backup.

The reason why I view the welfare state so deadly is in its deception, it lulls almost everyone to sleep until it is too late. In its early and middle stage almost everyone is fat and happy while it slowly eats away and destroys the nuclear family foundation and the very things that allow a society to survive. And In the final stage nothing can stop its inflationary spiraling from spinning out of control.

The billion dollar question is what is the wisest course to take out of this dilemma? This is my opinion and advice: The first priority is to save the federal government at all cost. To me that mean the government must slowly start jettisoning its social provider role and all other financial burdens through privatization, except the bare necessities.

It should slowly start privatizing out of all nonessential government burdens except the department of defense, treasure, interior, and one or two others. And above all, lower taxes not higher taxes are the only way out. To me that is the wisest course to take if this country is to have a fighting chance to survive. Sure, you can call me insane, a fool, a nut case or whatever, but that is my opinion and advice. No one is forced to believe me.

There really is no choice, because Mother Nature is cocked and ready to enforce its own law of "The survival of the strongest and the fittest" any day now. You can take my exceptional great wisdom with a grain of salt, or you can take it to the bank, It is out of my hand, I've did my duty.

The founding fathers knew what an all powerful government would do; they had seen it in old Europe. With the constitution they did all they could to enact laws to keep out of the driver's seat a government of unlimited power. Fast forward to today. The tenth amendment is totally ignored.

And I for one don't believe the constitution ever allowed for this almost unlimited taxing power the welfare state has today. It's over folks, the welfare state now has unlimited taxing power to support its super provider role. All we can do is pray and hope for the best.

After hearing a heated discussion on the radio involving the word "Hope" I decided to throw in my two cents. Beliefs like faith, hope, desire, etc. standing alone is practically useless. Anyone living only on faith or hope will die fasting.

However, the key or secret is to add another entirely different ingredient to the mix, that ingredient is "action." Then there is no greater force or power on earth than faith, hope, and courage in action. That is why we had better hurry up and get our act together or it won't be us that inherit the earth, we and all of western civilization may be on our knees praying several times a day.

On another subject, my experience is never let anyone make you an extreme perfectionist. It dehumanizes you. Race baiters and those that will never accept you will find something, if it's not this, it will be that. But, they can never mentally destroy you unless you hate them back. In the end, genuine good and decent people will accept you for who you are and what you are.

Sometimes until a storm passes over, repeating to yourself "May God bless him/her," and mean it, is the Christian thing to do. Fault finders will never stop finding flaws and caring and forgiving people will never stop loving. Balance is the key to life, and never an extreme.

Lately I hear the term "Protect the Children" and we know what is best for the children. In my view it is like "The three blind men examining an elephant." I can't remember all of the details, but all three came away with a different conclusion, one thought the legs were tree trunks. From a big picture point of view it is impossible for the welfare state to truly protect the children.

Until recently, going back over five thousand years the children were always protected because of one simple fact, the parents needed them for survival. Today most parents see children as love items to be pampered and doted upon. Kids are almost never seen as future meal tickets, which they are. The welfare state has taken away the need for the male head of household and the need to raise children like ones life will depends on it.

The supreme natural law of human survival is based on a survival need, and bleeding heart do good liberals have all but destroyed any need for responsibility, accountability, or anything else. I'm totally against any abuse of any child for any reason, period. God save us.

AN AFRICAN AMERICAN ANALYSIS

Overall the African Americans psyche and mentality has changed very little since slavery. The African American hue ranges from ebony black to almost Lilly white, but overall we still have a white identity mentality. Subconsciously African Americans still perceive black to be dependent and inferior to the preferred white master authority. As a race today; we still subconsciously see our black brothers as competitors and the enemy in winning white master authority approval

FREDDIE L. SIRMANS, SR'S LOG: 23 AUGUST 2009, 2051 HOURS.

World wide the welfare state system is on the brink of destroying western civilization. It destroys a nation's culture, its morals, its family values, and any capacity to barter. But, nothing has been more devastated by the welfare state than the African American community in the USA.

The African American people in America have come a long ways. The African American people survived slavery, racism, and unbelievable odds to now have a biracial black man in the white house. A great deal of the credit must go to all Americans because only in America could this happen.

America is still the greatest and all Americans have so much to be proud of. I write what I think and feel and pull very few punches. I'm old enough and remember when I went to an all black high school and violence on campus was something almost unheard of.

I remember as a teenager when there were teen clubs and soda shops where teens could dance and hang out all over town. Now, there are none because there is too much drug use and violence. I remember when teens had almost complete respect for authority.

Now, a five year old will cuss you out. So, what changed? What happen? What went wrong? I'll tell you, the "New Deal and the welfare state" seized the family provider role for itself, that's what went wrong. It seized the provider role and refused to enforce responsibility and accountability in raising the young that came with it.

Once the black man was kicked out of the house there was no one to instill "Self-restraint" in young black males. Those two words "Self-restraint" and the lack of it is why there is so much violence in the African American community. And the welfare state is what destroyed the black nuclear family and community.

All of the young gang banger and others that are committing so much senseless violence has never been conditioned to exercise self-restraint. Consequences in most cases are the furthest thing from a thugs mind. They have never been conditioned to expect swift and sure punishment for wrong doing.

As human we all at times get angry and frustrated, but someone with self-restraint don't just fly of the handle. Someone that has been taught self-restraint as a child is highly unlikely to just strike out with senseless violence.

Sure, almost every human being is capable of committing a violent act if provoked enough, but that is not the case with young black males. They are killing each other at the drop of a hat at an alarming rate all over the country.

The culture mentality must be shaped very young then eighteen years later you will have a productive responsible human being; otherwise you will keep producing die hard gang bangers with a destructive mentality. I think one of the biggest problems in the black community is we don't know who our friends are.

In the end no one is going to save the black

community except itself. However, it is about control, who exercises control. Anybody getting fed up and wanting to get tough and throw all of drug dealers and bad guys out is going to run up against the system.

This is America we are ruled by law, but that don't mean a community has to roll over and give up. Good and decent people always have the advantage, because at heart all people want to be thought of as good and decent. That is why culture is the most important thing of all for survival.

I don't care if you can't find but one or two decent people in a whole community those two should bond and shun all corruption. That is how decent people get and exercise control in their community, the wheat must be separated from the chaff meaning the good must be separated from the bad or one apple will spoil the whole barrel.

And there should be no exceptions unless one meets the minimum standards. To me it is the dumbest and silliest thing when supposedly intelligent African Americans wonder why taxicabs don't want to stop for blacks and why many people distrust young black males.

Hell, black taxicab drivers don't want to pick up black males, grow up and take responsibility, and I'm going to keep loving all people No matter who hates or disagrees with me. A community must separate itself from the rotten or the whole batch will be tainted in some way that is not just me saying it, that is reality.

All it takes is for decent people to set a standard, bond, and help and support each other, and hang tough. The corrupted must be shunned with no exception, which is not easy to do because everyone no matter how unfit is somebody's son, daughter, brother, sister, mom, dad, aunt, uncle, grandmother, grand dad, etc.

If a high standard is maintained everyone will soon want what you have. But, the system will chew you up and spit you out if there is ever a hint of violence to keep anyone out. The bad guys don't give a damn about obeying any law.

You can't beat them at their game, and they can't beat you at yours if you shun them stick together and stay the course. God save our African American community.

PS: Folks, like I keep repeating, its culture, culture, culture, and more culture, meaning a lack of it. There is no denying the fact proportional wise there is more African Americans babies being killed in the womb than anywhere in the world, Lord help us.

I think there is a phenomenon in the human psyche that I'm going to name "The master authority syndrome." I describe it as an awareness of who we perceive to be the master authority in our life. I believe it is something in our human makeup that aids our social survival. I believe nature programmed us to be aware of who is the master authority and to know ones place in the pecking order.

That is my theses, it is not based on any research or anything else, it's just my wisdom and observation. Now, let's apply it to the African American experience in America. African Americans were brought to America as slaves and stripped bare of their language and culture. Back in slavery from the beginning of the new African American psyche, it was drummed in that the white master authority was the only authority.

From a survival point of view African Americans had to keep aware of the white color of the master authority or be perceived as a threat. So, if a black face is mentally blocked from becoming an authority that locked blacks into a permanent dependent role. And one of the pitfalls of being a dependent is sibling rivalry for the approval of the master authority.

Overall the African Americans psyche and mentality has changed very little since slavery. The African American hue ranges from ebony black to almost Lilly white, but overall we still have a white identity mentality. Subconsciously African Americans still perceive black to be dependent and inferior to the preferred white master authority.

As a race today; we still subconsciously see our black brothers as competitors and the enemy in winning white master authority approval. We won't as a race help or support each other in business if there is a choice. Before the welfare state African Americans were slowly shedding their slavery baggage. Back then an all black neighborhood was the safest place a black person could be, but now it is the most dangerous place a black can be.

Back then blacks were very proud of their neighborhoods, some of the houses were run down but everyone took good care of what they had. Black business men were proud to locate in the black neighborhoods. Now, fast forward to today's African American mentality. If we didn't have a black identity biases why would our educated and elites want to get as far away as they can afford from an all black neighborhood.

Many will say the all black neighborhoods are too crime ridden, that may be true, but, blacks were fleeing well before rampant crime took over, the movie "A raising in the sun" proved that. Every other race will establish upper and middle class zones in and around their own community, why not African Americans? Sure, I may criticize African American rich and elites for deserting the black community, but the real true culprit that have destroyed our community pride and racial self-respect is the welfare state. Enough said, I think you get the point.

I know some may think I'm some kind of black separatist or anti-white hater, but nothing could be further from the truth. In fact I love white people and all people. I don't think Richard M. Nixon was far off the mark with some of the things he said about Africa. African Americans can learn to help and support each other and overcome this vicious sibling rivalry that is killing off so many of our young blacks.

The young African Americans don't know it, but subconsciously they are calling each other nigger and degrading an imaginary black faced rival and enemy that is inferior and doesn't deserve respect. Even though their face is the same color their own desired self image are white. The way out is to learn to love and respect all people. And here is a good formula, just repeat this quote until you learn it by heart. "I can wish all people goodwill through God which strengthens me."

One will never denigrate his immediate family

unless he doesn't feel a part of it. It is the same with ones own race family. One will not denigrate his race by using the hated "N" word unless he mentally doesn't feel part of something dear to him. That is because he doesn't mentally know who he is. But, of course there are a few who are ignorant and just don't give a damn. Also, I don't buy this loony idea that "you take the sting out of a degrading word by excess usage."

For African Americans to help and support each other the surest way would be to have a genuine survival need for each other, but that can't happen as long as we have this handout welfare state. "What the hell needs can a poor black man fill for a woman except stud service and companionship at her whim, when uncle sugar with his food stamps and countless social programs is her real provider and caretaker?"

To prove just how far this society has sunk, ninety five percent of the people in this country will think what I just said was sexist and insane. Only about five percent of the people left in this country will have the wisdom to know that what I just said is defending the nuclear family in the face of government abuse by liberal bleeding heart do-gooders.

Without the strong traditional nuclear family this country can't survive a nuclear blast, an economical collapse, or hardly anything. I double dog dare you! Prove me wrong! We have no bartering capacity left or food supplies on hand over a few days. And attacking me personally will prove nothing.

Unless this welfare state is dismantled and the nuclear family restored along with small farmers and home gardeners, this country and western civilization is doomed. What's going to happen when the dollar becomes worthless? Which won't be very much longer? You know something is terrible, terrible wrong when the rats are already secretly leaving the ship. All of these so called experts, especially women you see on TV with the gift of gab talking only rhetoric, they don't have a clue as to what it will take for this great nation to survive under distress.

In my view the freedom we now enjoy may be down to one decade left. I wouldn't be one bit surprised if within ten years the US will be ruled by some kind of civilian junta, following martial law. There is no doubt in my mind that it is only a matter of time before this big spending welfare state economy collapses. The president and congress should be trying to prepare and save the central government by jettisoning as many of its burdens' as possible. But, instead they are adding more and more big government program burdens.

They should be weaning people off the dole to

prepare them to survive on their own as much as possible without government. Believe it or not a survival need is what holds a society together. The reason the nuclear family is not supreme anymore is because big government spending took away the survival need for it.

Sure, if government start weaning people there are going to be a lot of hot air and real suffering and even deaths, but the good will far out weigh the bad by bringing back the strong nuclear family savior. That is the only way the US is going to be able to survive a nuclear attack or a collapsed economy, otherwise we can kiss this country goodbye.

When all is said and done, a civilization's survival depends on its offspring. The only true guarantee of a nation's survival is its parents raising responsible children to care for the parents when they are too old to care for themselves. There is no getting around this fact, unless you are one of the few very rich. The nuclear family is the only system know to man that can carry out this feat and guarantee lasting survival.
.

It seems the only time the people in this country are going to wake up is when the checks they receive will hardly buy a loaf of bread. Them all hell is going to break loose, there will be bottle necks everywhere, there will be rioting in the streets everywhere, and there will be starving and mass killings everywhere. And the masses of hungry undisciplined government dependents are going to feel what's yours is now theirs. The freedoms we now enjoy will be down the tube probably forever. As for me, I just hope I'm wrong on my predictions.

.

Mean while back to the subject, the only other way African Americans can help and support each other is through individual "Positive thinking." Just memorize the following quote and repeat it to yourself often, "I can wish all people goodwill through God which strengthens me." The answer to why African Americans vote overwhelming for one party has to do with a dependent mentality.

.

A parent can be a scheming phony, a two faced liar, and even worse, but as long as the kid (African America) is fed and not overly abused the kid is going to support that parent regardless. African Americans somewhere along the line perceived the democrat party as their white master authority parent.

.

It is like the unconditional love a mother has for her child. And the welfare state guarantees that African Americans and the poor stays dependent minded, thereby creating an emotional bond that cannot be broken, until these dependents are forced to grow up, stand on their own and make adult responsible choices.

.

.

Lately I hear the term "Protect the Children" and we know what is best for the children. In my view it is like "The three blind men examining an elephant." I can't remember all of the details, but all three came away with a different conclusion, one thought the legs were tree trunks. From a big picture point of view it is impossible for the welfare state to truly protect the children.

.

Until recently, going back over five thousand years the children were always protected because of one simple fact, the parents needed them for survival. Today most parents see children as love items to be pampered and doted upon. Kids are almost never seen as future meal tickets, which they are. The welfare state has taken away the need for the male head of household and the need to raise children like ones life will depends on it.

.

The supreme natural law of human survival is based on a survival need, and bleeding heart do good liberals have all but destroyed any need for responsibility, accountability, or anything else. I'm totally against any abuse of any child for any reason, period. God save us.

The old Du bois versus Booker T. Washington two schools of thought still haven't been settled and probably never will. Washington believed that African Americans should take the self reliance route and focus first on learning the basic trade vocations to feed and control their own destiny. He didn't put a priority on integration.

On the other hand, Du bois disagreed openly with Washington and believed that African Americans should not be limited in anyway. Du bois believed that blacks should go the full integration route and focus on the best education possibly. In my view the Du bois way was the right way in theory and it won out on the course blacks should take even to today.

But, as any scientist will tell you what works in theory doesn't necessarily work in practice. In almost all cases for any race to improve overall it must be pulled up from the top because those are the ones with the education and resources to make it happen. For many races there are no color differences, that way they can blend in and move into the mainstream very easily, no problem.

But, for African Americans the norm doesn't work in practice. The two main drawbacks are color difference and African American culture. In my view the biggest failure to uplift African

71

Americans have been the black elite by deserting the black community. Sure, crime and drugs are the excuse now, but that started long before crime and drugs were a big problem; just remember the movie "A raising in the sun."

I understand safety and the need for a pecking order, but blacks could establish middle and upper class zones in or on the edge of black communities if they wanted to. Also, blacks should open businesses and invest back in their own communities like all other races, but it's not happening on a large scale. I think It's something a lot deeper here that African Americans need to face and accept.

I think African Americans as a race are still running away from themselves and their communities. I don't think African Americans as a whole respect themselves unconditional as individuals and as a race with all the flaws and blemishes, unconditionally. I don't think most blacks have a do-for-your-self independent mentality that will make you respect yourself and people that look like you.

I think we as blacks need to face and accept one another with pride and nothing to prove, flawed and scarred but as good as anybody or any race, period. "We don't need a ticket to ride, or to qualify, no one asked to be born, just forgive and accept the past and move on." Do-for-your-self people don't worry about imaginary threats from the past or empty symbolisms; they are too busy working to live a proud independent dignified life.

No one can truly accept and respect you unless you first accept and respect yourself, unconditionally. The color different won't let blacks just blend into the mainstream unnoticed, plus, there is an unspoken negative stereotypical image of blacks as a whole. That unspoken image associates blacks as a whole with property devalue, social baggage, crime, and a few other negative stereotypes.

Still, genes are getting through because in my view big booties are no longer limited to African Americans. The culture drawback is far too many African Americans still unconsciously believe the old black stereotype that black is inferior (that the white man's beer is colder). Far too many blacks still see other blacks as competitors and the enemy in winning mainstream approval.

For that reason we tend not to support one another as a whole in business in the black communities like back in the nineteen forties and fifties.

Lately I hear the term "Protect the Children" and we know what is best for the children. In my view it is like "The three blind men examining an elephant." I can't remember all of the details, but all three came away with a different conclusion, one thought the legs were tree trunks. From a big picture point of view it is impossible for the welfare state to truly protect the children.

Until recently, going back over five thousand years the children were always protected because of one simple fact, the parents needed them for survival. Today most parents see children as love items to be pampered and doted upon. Kids are almost never seen as future meal tickets, which they are. The welfare state has taken away the need for the male head of household and the need to raise children like ones life will depends on it.
The supreme natural law of human survival is based on a survival need, and bleeding heart do good liberals have all but destroyed any need for responsibility, accountability, or anything else. I'm totally against any abuse of any child for any reason, period. God save us.

Well, for what it is worth I decided to add my two cents to the subject, "On the down low." It is no secret that AIDS is far out of proportion in the African American communities and even on Historically Black

74

Colleges and Universities (HBCUs). There must be a reason why this is so. I was the first one that pointed out that the revolving door in and out of the prison system was the leading factor. But, that still doesn't explain why this out of proportion also exists on HBCUs.

That means there must be a culture factor involved. Many believe it is how the African American community defines homosexuality. The general mainstream assumption is that anyone participating in a homosexual act is a homosexual, but that is not what many minority men believe. A great many minority men view homosexuality basically in the same light as masturbation. They view the act in terms of dominant or submission or driver or receiver.

They believe that as long as they are in the dominant role and doing the driving their manhood is not at issue or threatened. They feel they are only acting like a squirrel as long as it is kept secret. Whereas, it is only the one that is in the submissive and receiving role that makes one a homosexual. As a writer I'm not deciding anything, I'm just trying to shine as much light as possible on the true mindset.

To get at the AIDS problem, you first need to understand what people are really thinking. The fact is, it boils down to the same old saw, that is permissive sexual behavior and loose morals. Men have in the past and will always try to get easy sex from whoever will give it up. So, the ultimate AIDS solution lies with the women in this country. Women need to stop giving up all of this easy unobligated sex, period. And I put almost the entire blame on why they won't cross their legs on the welfare state.

Back before we had a super big government sugar daddy provider, very few African American women would give up easy sex without an obligated commitment, and even then he had to be of sound character. Back then If a suitor wouldn't go to church and clean up his act, it was "Her way or the highway," and she had a strong dad or brother that would kick butt to back her up. My solution as always gets the government the hell out of the family provider business.

In my opinion, AIDS in the African American community is approaching the out of control level. Now because of the vast improvement of new drug we don't hear much about AIDS anymore but still that don't mean it's gone away. There is still no cure and taking what is called a cocktail of drugs is no easy burden on the stomach.

The subject of prostitution is where you will find more hypocrites and self-righteousness than anywhere else. I'm not condoning anything, I'm just writing my views and observations. When you go back in history one thing all civilizations had in common was they had the wisdom to leave certain things alone. Prostitution was one of those things. It has always been legal and tolerated throughout history for a very good reason.

In fact, in my view it is shallow and stupid to make prostitution illegal, why do you think we have so many child molesters and all kinds of perverts? Sure, regulate it and keep it under control but it should never be made illegal. Mother Nature gave great pleasure to eating and sex to make sure there will be future generations. Therefore, those with real wisdom tend to leave prostitution alone as a necessary sin and not preach and fool around with it.

Prostitution is a venting mechanism that takes pressure off the good decent nuclear family way of life. There are certain things we can pretend to get rid of, but in reality we can't and still remain civilized. We may be human, civilized, and all that, but we still have animal instincts. Right now, there is more sneaking around after dark than most of us would like to believe. Sexual energy is no fantasy it is physical and real whether we like it or not.

It is one of the most powerful forces in our entire make up. Sexual energy will build up like pressure in a steel drum and if it is not vented in a harmless way society is going to pay a price. It's not something that can be snuffed out without serious side effects; sages of the distance past understood that. Just look around to where the force of some of this energy is popping out in perverted ways. There is a reason why the world's oldest profession is still around.

Many will strongly disagree with my observations on this, but in my view the oldest profession has always been and will always be a societal relief valve. It is a relief valve for the unmarried and many other situations. Common sense should tell you what happens when a relief valve is closed off. Men by nature are aggressive creatures and sometimes one slight touch or one show of affection will prevent total self-destruction.

As it is those that are ugly, antisocial, and with many other imperfections can't find legal sexual relief. Most men can channel their sexual energy into other productive things, but some cannot. Why do you think we have such a long list of child molesters and other perverts now days? My guess is unvented sexual energy is one leading cause. With no legal relief of sexual energy the only choice for many is self-relief.

To get sexual relief a lot of men have sold out their soul and true beliefs, then start believing their sold out views as fact, that is one reason why you see so many spineless men today. Most of us have seen cases where a young man stays in trouble and is out of control, and then he finds a girl friend or gets married and becomes as calm as a cucumber. Sure, he may feel more responsible, but the main reason is most of his aggression is being vented.

Capitalizing on self-sexual relief is what's behind and driving this whole out of control invasive video pornography sex industry. There may be a lot of lookers, but the ones actually spending big money and buying are viewing for masturbating purpose, which is supporting and allowing all of this sluttish invasive stuff to be in our face. Surprisingly, women make up almost half of these consumers. However, I got news for anyone watching too much pornography.

It can dull ones sexual imagination and lock one in a visual stimulation only mode in order to stay aroused. My intent is not to write how thing should or should not be, but to write things the way they really are. So, "How do you like me now?

Lately I hear the term "Protect the Children" and we know what is best for the children. In my view it is like "The three blind men examining an elephant." I can't remember all of the details, but all three came away with a different conclusion, one thought the legs were tree trunks. From a big picture point of view it is impossible for the welfare state to truly protect the children.

Until recently, going back over five thousand years the children were always protected because of one simple fact, the parents needed them for survival. Today most parents see children as love items to be pampered and doted upon. Kids are almost never seen as future meal tickets, which they are. The welfare state has taken away the need for the male head of household and the need to raise children like ones life will depends on it.

The supreme natural law of human survival is based on a survival need, and bleeding heart do good liberals have all but destroyed any need for responsibility, accountability, or anything else. I'm totally against any abuse of any child for any reason, period. God save us.

This subject reminds me of the vacationing tourist that walked up to a local that had his feet propped up and was kicked back under a tree. The tourist asked the man, "Why don't you get up and get a job?" The local said, "For what?" "To make money." "Make money for what," said the local? "So you can relax, enjoy yourself, and take it easy later in life."

The local said, "Why bother I'm already doing all that." The point I'm trying to make is what really matters in life is food, shelter, and the basics for a comfortable life. It matters not if one makes a hundred dollars a day if one can't afford enough food, shelter, warmest, and the basic comforts of life.

In my view protecting the culture and producing enough food to survive should always be the first priorities for any country. The surest way to destroy any country is to take away its struggle to survive, period. When the struggle to survive goes, so goes individual accountability and responsibility followed by disrespect for authority, moral decay, crime, drug, and on and on.

In my view any poor country that has great wealth in natural resources or by any other means should use a dual track economy. What I mean by dual track is always keep the great wealth income completely separated to be spent only on infra structural, and never to be use for handouts. In fact stay away from hand outs, period, if you want to save your culture, handouts is a white man's disease.

I don't believe there is a poor country anywhere that couldn't feed itself on its own if the government would allow producers to keep ninety percent of all profit. There would be entrepreneurs springing up almost overnight to fill the need, but those governments would never keep hand off higher taxes, no way.

The other day I was listening to this commentator and he asked something to this effect, "Can you prove that we are not the most intelligent beings in the universe." I thought about that and decided to ponder the question. I'm not sure if I or anyone can prove it but I know there is a higher power, you can call him God, Jehovah, Allah, A superior being, or whatever. You see, we are in a mental box called logic.

We are locked in and cannot escape. With only logic we will never be able to understand the beginning of our existence or our purpose here on earth. Logic dictates that there had to be a beginning at some point in time, which makes it impossible to ever understand our existence with only logic. The actual facts are man doesn't truly know what time or existence mean. Example: Computers are locked in a binary system and cannot escape.

Computers respond only to a negative or a positive polarity. Super computers are super fast but they still can't get past the binary system. Our five senses connects us to reality, otherwise there would be no reality. Does that mean there would still be reality if no life could sense it? Like the old question: "If a tree fell in the Forrest and there were nothing or no body there to hear it, would there be a sound?"

Who knows, in time other senses could evolve to produce a higher level of intelligent. There are animals that have senses that can match almost anything we can do with modern technology and probably countless other things we haven't discovered and are not aware of. There are animals that have senses of radar, sonar, electricity, and many other things that modern technology can and cannot do.

Who knows, there may be infinite worlds and dimensions coexisting with us that we don't have the senses to detect. Who knows how Nessie and Bigfoot come and goes. In most of the animal world smell is the dominant sense and is many, many times more powerful than ours. Down wind a polar bear can smell prey almost a hundred miles away. It is almost unbelievable what a blood hound can do with the sense of smell.

Logic dictates that there must be a beginning to everything. Just think of the old riddle, "Which came first, the chicken or the egg?" Being boxed in with logic we can't even solve a simple little riddle like that. But, we know the answer must lie somewhere. We understand relativity; nothing doesn't just happen with no connection. In closing, wise men realized long ago that our power to reason was limited, so for the sake of sanity there must be a deity or deities with all the answers.

I totally agree. Wait, hold on a moment, I've decided to delve deeper into this chicken and egg riddle. Actually there is no such thing as which came first in the "Which came first, the chicken or the egg riddle." The chicken or the egg riddle is actually a life cycle circuit which is a unit of one. No matter how many parts a circuit has it still operates as one unit. My observation of the unit of one oneness opens up far deeper questions, but I will leave it there for now.

Sure, life can evolve and adapt, but, a beginning life cycle circuit must be made, powered, maintained, and exist for some purpose. We humans don't make electrical circuits without some purpose.

WILL CHAOS DESTROY THE UNITED STATES?

Every financial-burden the USA government takes on will be paid out of the profit margin of private businesses because there won't be any wages paid to employees to be taxed unless that business first make a profit. And as the government takes more and more of their profit, fewer and fewer businesses will have enough profit left to survive on, let alone hire more workers. After 80 years of sugar daddy government spending we have finally reached a saturation point.

FREDDIE L. SIRMANS SR'S LOG: 15 NOVEMBER 2009, 1131 HOURS
THE BIG TRIAL IN NEW YORK CITY.
THIS IS AN OFF SUBJECT BULLETIN: Let me throw my two cent worth in here. In my mind there is no limit to how shallow liberals can be. Protect New York City from what! Sure the trial is going to go on and definitely will be protected.

But, it is the roll of the dice and is opening up a can of worms. Can New York City protect every store, hotel, mall, rail road, and on and on like in Tel Aviv. Why invite the unknown, lets just hope my extreme caution is just pesky nonsense.

GITMO AND WATER BOARDING!
For some reason those two subjects just won't get out of the limelight. For some reason the liberals just won't let go and let sleeping dogs lie. They just keep fueling the fire and boiling this dirty linen in public when matter like this should be settled at the highest levels behind closed doors.

I can't predict the future and no one can, but I think there is an even chance this sleeping dog may end up biting a bunch of liberals. When I turn on the TV all I hear is Gitmo, Gitmo, all day long. For me to meddle in an issues of this type is unpredictable and may even be dangerous, but, as a writer I just couldn't take it any longer, I just had to put pen to paper, so be it.

Now, here is my ounce of wisdom, you can take it with a grain of salt or you can take it to the bank. As I kick back in my recliner and listen to the liberals and others talk, the main thing they are focusing on is how secure the maximum security prisons are and that nobody has ever escaped.

They are not even in the ballpark on the danger of closing Gitmo and bringing those prisoners here. Of course, I'm not one bit surprised because I think most liberals are shallow and lack real wisdom. In fact it is not just the liberals, the welfare state has made nearly 90 percent of the American population shallow and hype prone, over a hundred million people voted for the American idol winner.

The mostly liberal media is so bias against anything conservative that they wouldn't tell you even if they did see a closing Gitmo threat, which they don't. Very few Americans actually see the big picture here. I may be wrong but I believe if Gitmo is closed and those people are brought here on American soil we will have a whole new ball game.

I believe this whole life or death struggle we are locked in will be ratcheted up several notches. Let's just say one member of a family clan is being held for whatever reason and the rest of the family members know where he is being held, do you think the rest of the family is going to forget him and stay far, far away?

No, we are dealing with people that has no fear of death, and I will bet they will create moles and try to get as close as possible. I don't know what will happen and no on does but you can rest assured if you put those people here on American soil the sky will be the limit. I'm just one lone writer expressing my grave concerns.

Gitmo is on an island surrounded by water which makes it extremely hard to get to, plus it is not even our territory. But, all of that will change if you bring those people here on the North American mainland. If the ante is raised by bringing those people here on American soil, nothing may not happen, but, we better be prepared to guard our malls and everything else like never before.

Folks, I'm a self-made writer and great thinker, I'm not even right half of the time, and I may be just making a mountain out of a mole hill. So, never mind me, just go on about your business and forget you even read this article. Phil. 4-13 I can do all things through God which strengthens me.

FREDDIE L. SIRMANS, SR'S LOG: 14 MAY 2009, 1215 HOURS

As I have said before a "Welfare State" is the most dangerous and destructive form of government to ever exist in the history of civilization. No other form of government exist that will completely rip the nuclear family system apart and make it impossible for that society to survive long term.

It destroys the sense of self-responsibility and accountability in people, it kills a strong survival instinct and lulls people into a love, love false sense of security, and then drives the final nail in by breeding people that is asleep and don't have the character or judgment to recognize a moral or any other threat until the wolf is at the door.

The following are the things every society must have to survive and it destroys every last one of them. There is very little left of our once strong nuclear and extended family system, especially among African Americans, you can now wipe the floor with our once strong morals and values code, and our once breadbasket Midwest small farmers along with the rest of the nation's small farmers and home gardeners that got us through the great depression is long gone.

We have almost no emergency fallback bartering capacity to keep this nation alive during a calamity. We as a people are at freedoms death door and it is so sad that still far too many people are more concerned about who is starring in Hollywood. I believe the government need to snap out of its denial, face reality and start planning how to survive through an inevitable collapse.

The nation needs to start planning masses of food kitchens, masses of food shelter programs, masses of medical clinics, and when that is completed junk the minimum wage and cut all taxes to the bone across the board. Then, the free market place will save itself and the country, too, if the government as designed will stays with protecting the country and let the economy sinks or swims on its own. No one wants this solution, but reality is reality.

This way, at least we will be in control, and even then we will have only a fighting chance to save our nation and freedom. Folks, I'm a writer and I write what I think and believe, no one has to believed me or take me serious. In truth, I, myself, hope I'm wrong on what I think.

Of course, I don't expect the powers that be to even consider a hard decision like this; they will continue to take the liberal course of least resistance. I expect the powers that be to make deals around the world and finish selling off what little is left of the soul of America.

FREDDIE L. SIRMANS, SR'S LOG: 13 MAY 2009, 1530 HOURS

A lot of good citizens look at the condition of America and wonder when and where did we go wrong. I, Freddie L. Sirmans, Sr. will tell you when we the citizens lost control of this great country. It was around eighty years ago when we allowed the government to seize the traditional nuclear family provider role for itself.

You see, whoever is in the provider role is the boss and calls the shots. Instead of going into a lot of elaborating I will just get to the point. What started off initially as a small "New Deal" provider baby has over time grown into this huge monster size welfare state beast. Now the appetite of this ferocious beast is gobbling up every tax dollar or any other dollar that it can seize.

I believe it is futile and we are deluding ourselves to think we can save our economy and freedom as long as this beast is in the social and family provider role. This beast favors low values and loose morals and sees self-sufficiency as a threat to its power and that will not be tolerated.

We have this beast loose upon the land with unlimited taxing power, and that means no one in this country is safe from unreasonable taxes. Unless this beast is neutered and downsized out of its super provider role I think trying to save the economy and the country is a waste of time and resources. God save America.

BOOK SELLING WORLD SHUNS FREDDIE L. SIRMANS, SR'S BOOKS

I don't know how it is done, but, I believe the book selling world has an unwritten rule that prevents books by an extreme conservative neurotic like me from being sold. I can't prove it but I feel there may be a hidden hand somewhere preventing me from selling more books. Sure, some of the grammar is crude and incorrect to some degree; still the people should make that choice.

I believe a super great thinker and writer like me deserve to be selling books in the thousands. Now! Take that unwritten rule! Invisible hand! The name Freddie L. Sirmans, Sr. is out there, it is all over the internet. No one can convince me that there is not an opposing force that doesn't want it known what is in Freddie L. Sirmans' Books.

If nothing else, someone is going to buy just to see what is going on. Just because I'm saying it doesn't mean nothing is there. Just because someone is paranoid doesn't mean they are not in danger. Believe it or not, paranoid people live longer. There is no one alive today that better articulates in simple terms the inner working of how an economy should work.

I lay it out so simple that even an idiot can understand it. However, history has proven that one of the hardest things there is is to keep a genuine good man down. There is a destiny reason why a poor neurotic uneducated South Georgia USA country boy can reach out and grab the imaginary reins of the U.S. Economy, yank back and yell "Whoa" before it goes over the cliff. Praise be to God. Amen.

A word of knowledge to any conservative with his head above the crowd, the liberals may come after you with extra venom because of misplaced aggression. I'm the wanted target but that is out of the question. No liberal is going to make famous in their minds a nobody neurotic nut case. I have no hate or dislike for liberals in fact I think they are great Americans, but shallow and shouldn't control our destiny.

I consider myself a realist not a conservative. I love my country and as long as I have the freedom to write my views I'm going to say what I believe to be best for the long term survival of my country. I believe great character and good judgment goes hand in hand. And I believe great or good character can only come from some form of real or imposed struggle in life.

It is not just the liberals that lack the character to make sound judgment; we can't put all of the blame for the destruction of our culture and nuclear family system on them. I may be screwed up and unknown, but the liberals know I'm a deadly threat because I am striking at the heart of their false God, the "Welfare State." And in their eyes anyone that does that with a wallop is a mortal enemy.

I keep pounding body blows to their soft underbelly and sooner or later it's going to tally. The liberals know this and are counter punching by going after any high profile conservative they can sink their teeth in. This misdirected aggression is only going to increase. They won't dare focus attention on me because they feel the less people know what I'm writing the better.

My writing is based on logic and common sense and just like the saying goes, "The proof of the pudding is in the eating. And in this case the proof of the writing is in the reading." Throughout nature and survival there will always be an exception to everything. Having said that, anyone with genuine sound character and judgment will by instinct know that abortions and gay marriages are a threat to long term survival.

Exceptions are part of nature and those that are affected should be loved and respected, but a spade is a spade no matter what political correction says. I will say that less than five percent of the entire U.S. Population has the judgment today to even believe how close this nation is to total destruction as a free people. I have no need or desire to try to scare anyone, but as a writer I have a duty to share my wisdom and knowledge if it will help save this great nation.

I see a dire future, but the future is never set in stone, man always has the ability to determine his own future by his own actions.

PS: We have here high drama, stay tuned. You don't want to miss anything.

Where do most citizen tax payers get their money, from their small business employers? Where do all businesses get their money, from citizen customers, some of which they themselves employ. As you can see the economy operates as a giant cycle Human energy and intelligence creating something of value in the form of food and resources is what keeps this cycle going. And the rewarding byproduct of the whole process is what's called profit. That is what government takes, all taxes ultimately comes from some form of profit.

Sure, government needs a certain amount of

profit driven tax money to protect the nation from both foreign and domestic enemies and basic interior needs. But, the USA government was never designed to be a cradle to grave social and family provider.

Now, big government at all levels is taking far too much of small businesses profit for many of them to survive let alone hire anyone. And you gonna tell me mass tax cuts to the bone is not the answer, go fly a kite!!!

I'm over whelmed sometimes as a writer to just take a moment to examine who I am or what I am about To others my whole personality is almost totally misunderstood like a facade Even those close to me misunderstand why I am a loner or keep mostly to myself no matter the reason I tell themi
Human beings are by nature social creatures and any time they are not it is because of fear, guilt, or shame somewhere in their past. There are some things in life that can only be understood from personal experience. I experience the high joys and happiness's a lot, but, I believe I have had more than my share of the emotional pain and despair lows.

I'm a very spiritual person that doesn't practice religion as much as I should, there is a difference. Improvement is admitted. However, as I get older, more and more I'm beginning to think that those that say "God has a purpose for each of us" has a point. I believe in life nothing is completely free, there is some price for everything we do.

I don't have the answer, but I do know I have paid a very heavy mental price practical all of my life. And I wonder why, why oh Lord. I would never wish my lifetime mental struggles on anyone even though it has rewarded me with almost super natural wisdom. Maybe there is something to this thing called "Destiny."

You can think anything you please about my state of mind because I know it is impossible for anyone to go insane as long as he/she can show love and forgiveness to all no matter how he is treated in return. Yet, I still don't understand why would an uneducated handicapped neurotic like me be given so much raw wisdom and power by destiny. Yes, power to influence because you are now reading this. God I ask in your name save this USA great nation, the land of the free and the home of the brave.

PS: With love to you always from me, Freddie L. Sirmans, Sr. himself, who has bared his inner soul? Thank you.

Folks, I'm here to tell you, I don't think the American people realize the dire circumstance we are dealing with. We are dealing with a welfare state beast with almost total power. It didn't take this power; the American voters kept voting the same pie in the sky liberals back into office.

This welfare state beast has tasted the power of being a super provider and now it will never give up even one inch. And you couple that with an almost unlimited power to tax, and then you have a beast that has the power to take whatever it pleases. So, I'm forewarning you, you just watch, this beast is not going to let the constitution or any law stop it from having its way.

First, unless we de-claw and destroy this beast while we still can, we the American people might as well kiss our freedom and country goodbye. I'm telling you, this beast has almost total power and its going to boil down to it or us. Right now this beast is only flexing its muscles, you wait, and you haven't seen anything, yet. Anywhere there is money in this country it is only a matter of time before this beast finds a way to take it.

So, I'm telling you this beast must be taken down now before it obtains absolute power. If we wait, you just watch, it is going to chew up the five freedoms in the constitution and spit them out. Oh mighty God I ask in your name, save the great United States of America.

I believe more and more people are viewing me, Freddie L. Sirmans, Sr. as a great thinker. Myself, I certainly think I'm a great thinker even if no one else does. In the field of economics I haven't studied or read hardly anything on the subject, but, about forty years ago I seen in a pamphlet that "All economies start with bartering."

That was all it took for my great thinking ability to take it from there and understand how economics in its relationship to motivation in tune with the laws of nature like "Natural selection" played out. Even today almost everyone thinks America's biggest problem is the economy, wrong. A bad or even a collapsed economy could never bring down a great nation with a strong culture and moral code in place.

The economy is just one leg of the human survival stool. The other three legs are number one, culture with good morals and values, number two, a strong nuclear family system, and number three, a minimum fall back emergency bartering capacity utilizing small farmers and home gardeners. The welfare state has destroyed all of that; all we have left is a sugar daddy welfare state with millions upon millions solely dependent on it for survival.

The Roman Empire lasted a thousand years and nothing since has even come close to that. Since the come about of fiat money around forty years ago culture has gotten lost in the shuffle, before then culture and values stayed on the front burner to keep nations and individuals living within their means. Culture is what really protects a nation and its way of life.

Fiat money has allowed the welfare state to corrupt our once strong culture and moral values to the point that now "If it feels good do it." Someone with a super strong survival instinct like me belongs in the zoo or some place like that according to political correctness, how sad. It is never too late, we still have time to cut taxes to the bone and relearn to depend and rely on our self's instead of big government.

Otherwise, Mother Nature is going to discipline us and it won't be pretty; there may not be a one United States again, ever. God save the great United States of America.

Even Mother Nature herself is not out there just free wheeling it. Nature operates on set laws and principals with just a few we know of. Thanks to Darwin who was the first to recognize nature's law of "Natural selection." There is a natural law of "The survival of the strongest and the fittest." And the "Tendency to take the course of least resistance" even applies to things like electricity.

However, there is nothing in nature completely absolute; there is an exception to everything. That is why in nature things will happen that seem impossible to the human mind. To the human mind even our existence itself is impossible. We are like human computers programmed with logic, we are boxed in with our intelligence limited to only logic. With only logic it is impossible for us to ever understand our existence.

Logically speaking there must be a God, a superior being, or infinite levels of intelligence. Sorry, I just got a little carried away in my brainstorming.

Before the "New Deal" started our welfare state the American people respected the laws of nature. They knew one rotten apple would spoil the barrel. People don't think of it that way but that old saying is really a law of nature. How can the United States think it can prosper when it ignores so many of the laws of nature? If one doesn't pay for his own sins we all will end up paying like the rest of the apples in a barrel.

ILLEGAL DRUG WAR TACTIC.
In one of my book almost twenty years ago in jest I gave this simple solution for dealing with illegal drugs, change the currency. But now, it presents a greater opportunity to kill two birds with one stone. Most street transactions for illegal drugs are twenty

dollars or less. So, why not just phase out the 5, 10, and 20 dollar paper bills, with 5, 10, and 20 dollar coins with their value in itself in precious metals.

It would be the wisest thing this government could do because the paper dollar is going to become worthless anyway. Sure, it would be a terrible inconvenience for businesses, but a nightmare for drug dealers trying to hide their illegal profits. Besides, most people use checks, debit cards, or credit cards anyway. However, I don't expect this tactic to be taken seriously, I just felt like doing a little brainstorming anyway, who knows, it may provoke thoughts to a real solution.

Originally all currency had its value in itself. The currency consisted of precious metals like gold and silver. With the price of copper today a pure copper penny would certainly be worth more than one cent. If the value of our money was in the money itself the welfare state couldn't just inflate the people's wealth out of existence.

Anyone holding paper that represents wealth may not be wealthy six months from today the way things seems to be headed. Laws or anything else on paper are no stronger than the culture and moral values backing them up. I'm telling you now our welfare state beast is master and no law or anything else is going to stop politicians from feeding this beast.

The real solution is to starve this beast to death, it lives on tax money, but, it may too late now half of the country wants this beast to live and take care of them. Who knows, I may be the same as David but with a pen.

IS IT REAL OR FANTASY?
Like the movie when the villain comes out of the computer into real life, it seems the government has stolen the kid's monopoly game and took their money. What is the difference? The government now just prints money as it sees fit; money no longer represents spent human energy resulting from blood, sweat, and tears.

If the government wants to buy park place or boardwalk it just prints what it need and make the purchase. We all know monopoly is a make believe kids game, but now it has come out of fantasy land into real life in terms of U.S. currency.

When will we wake up from this dream? My God! Stop, stop the tape! Let's snap out of this insanity! Doesn't anyone have an ounce of wisdom anymore? "Send in the clowns." Hallelujah! Long live the king! The show is over, let's go home. Is this fact or fiction? The end is near.

PS: Folks, in case you are wondering about

my sanity, I know a guaranteed way how not to ever go off the deep end and lose touch with reality. Never forget that it is impossible for anyone to go crazy or insane as long as he can genuine love and forgive others, no matter how he is treated in return, I can. Yours truly, by Freddie L. Sirmans, Sr.

THE LIBERALS NOW HAVE THE POWER FOR THE TAKE DOWN.

I heard this question the other day; will they ever address Washington's spending? I decided to give my answer to that question, my answer is no. This is my reasoning on why, there is no limit to man's desires and self-interest, but, there is always a physical barrier somewhere to stop him. The gold standard done that! The gold standard was the physical barrier that disciplined a nation by purging out anti-survival threats to the culture and moral values.

The thing that very few today has the wisdom to understand is money is not the thing that determines whether a nation survives or perishes. Peoples and societies survived for thousands of years even before money was invented and even through the great depression when very few people had any. The liberals could never have destroyed this nation before the new deal and social programs begin because the culture and moral values were much too strong, their frontier like spirit wouldn't have put up with it.

No, the free handout to buy vote had to first corrupt the nations culture, morals, and family values first. Now, the liberals have the power for the take down! I think far too many people are too shallow to recognize a moral or survival threat when they see it. The wolf is at the door and most people don't even know it, their faith is in uncle sugar.

I understand why people think I don't care when I call for draconian tax cuts and eliminating farm subsidies. That is because I have the wisdom to know beyond a shadow of doubt that the people must relearn to depend on themselves for this nation to survive. Mass tax cuts across the board would restore our culture, morals, and family values. No amount of money is going to save this nation. Only forced relearning to survive on our own as individual units is going to do that.

God save this great nation, it is in your hand.

A THOUGHT FOR THE DAY:
"Hell has no fury like a woman scorned." Well, I could be wrong, but I suspect at some point soon the liberals will find that "Hell has no fury like a free press waking up and seeing the light." I suspect the "Free press" is among the living and still wants to survive, too. The coffee sure smells great.

ECONOMICAL SUCCESS IS IMPOSSIBLE WITH GOVERNMENT INVOLVEMENT! The biggest misconception that almost everyone including economist have today is the government can manage a successful economy, false. Government never has and never will be able to manage a successful economy that can feed its entire people. There is a tried and true economical ideology that have proven time after time that it always work, except for one thing, the government has to get the hell out of the way and stay the hell out of the way.

That ideology is "allow free competition and let the free market place work." That ideology will always work and produce more food than the country can eat and an abundance of everything else. The reason governments will never be able to manage a successful economy is there is just too many variables and many of them are subjective.

To name just a few of the many variables that will derail a successful economy, they are, who you know, who gets hurt, who has power, and who is under the desk, stop, disregard that last one, how did that get in there? When allowed to "A genuine free market place" will use a natural selection process better known as supply and demand to create a balance between the merchant and the consumer. The natural selection process is not hindered by subjective feeling and emotions and will weed out waste, inefficiency, and unproductively.

However, government management is just the opposite; it is all about favoritism thereby rewarding the inefficient and unproductive. To sum it up, government should stay with what it does best, collect taxes due and protect the country. If left alone the merchants and consumes will adhere to a natural selection process and untold wealth will be produced by entrepreneurs for all. It is not the amount of money that counts it is the buying power that counts; under the gold standard $5.00 in the past would buy more than fifty dollars today.

There is a reason why most of the world is poor and will always be poor, the government has the power and the gun and will not stay out of the way. Sure, the poor will always need help, but that should be the role of the nuclear family, the extended family, the church, and social organizations. Amen brother.

WHY KEEP FEEDING THE WELFARE STATE BEAST?

Me, I've never pretended to be unbiased. I classify myself to be a realist, or even an extremist throwback. In my personal opinion I view liberals with total power like a kid behind the wheel, and even scarier is they are now in charge of the candy store. I believe that the only thing that truly matters to them is feeding the "Welfare state beast" that they have created along with some liberal republicans. It is to hell with the survival of the country or anything else.

It is not because they don't give a damn. They really do care; they are genuine bleeding hearts with other people's money. I love all people including liberals, they are good Americans, and truly mean well. It's just that they are shallow and don't know it due to the lack of any true life or death survival struggle. It's not all their fault, the welfare state breeds them. I just don't believe liberals have the depth or wisdom to handle total power.

For years the liberals have been experts at shifting and placing blame. Now, all you hear is bipartisanship. The reason is the liberals know that their shell game without the pea will be exposed if they go it alone. That's what all of the bipartisanship ruckus is about. They don't need but two or three liberals from the opposition that they can easily pick up, but, oh no, there must be bipartisanship. If they thought the voter would buy their raw exposed ideology they would gladly go it alone.

A hundred years ago probably the only place

you could find a liberal would be in a rich family or maybe on a collage campus. Today liberals run academia and control most institutions in America. God save America.

COLD STEEL REALITY IS LURKING OUT THERE SOMEWHERE

From time to time through out history individuals and nations has had to rediscover a basic law of nature, that law is "There are no free rides ultimately someone always pay one way or another." Life can become unrealistic in terms of dreams, fantasies, eliminating all pain and suffering and on and on, but the one thing that always brings us back to ground is cold steel reality. Sometimes pain and suffering is the only thing that will get people's attention.

Without some hardship along with pain and suffering we all would lose sight of reality and self destruct. With this global economy nonsense it looks like the whole world is going to have to rediscovery this basic law of nature. However, it looks like the liberals in America are getting everything they can while the getting is good as if there is no tomorrow.

After years of running their shell game successful the liberals have finally hit the jack pot. They have created enough "Expecting something for nothing dependent minded voter" to get almost everything they want. It does look like the Lib's are now unstoppable, but, never forget that rock hard cold steel reality is lurking out there somewhere. There is no such thing as "Something for nothing" in this world. God save America

UPDATE: Anybody that thinks this new stimulus package is going to save us is in for a very rude awakening. All it is going to do is make the "Cost of living boogie man" angrier. It is going to be like adding a JTO (Jet assisted takeoff) bottle to the galloping cost of living and bring the buying power of the dollar down two extra notches. I believe nothing short of mass across the board tax cuts is going to save the dollar from being worth less than the paper it is printed on, eventually.

CAUTION: Stop! Don't read this article! Take my advice! Trust me! You are going to read it anyway, so, do it at your own risk. I'm going to do some real thinking out loud here and it ain't going to be pretty. I'm going to imagine what is in the heads of the economists running the whole show. These people are very intelligent with lot of knowledge on doing what they do.

These guys know that I'm probably right on saying the "galloping cost of living" is the real problem that is destroying the economy. But, just even mentioning that as a problem is taboo in economic circles. Just the thought of dealing with something like that will leave economist shaking in their boots because of the dreaded "D" word and that is the last thing they want to even mention.

The biggest difference between them and me is these guys think they can out smart and cheat Mother Nature, I don't. They think they can put off the day of reckoning forever, I don't. These people are not dumb; they know we can't keep borrowing and printing worthless money but only so long. But they are in a state of denial with no one wanting to face or deal with the dreaded "D" word.

We are now almost down to day to day economical survival. The liberal with their created welfare state has produced millions upon millions of government dependents that can't survive if the government runs out of cash, so the presses press on. Anyone with an ounce of common sense knows it can only end is disaster, yet the presses drone on. We are only following suit.

Never in history has a nation knowing it is headed toward disaster changed course. I'm telling you now the die is cast, the "Cost of living boogie man" and the dwindling buying power of the dollar can't be ignored, and that is what's taking this nation down. Deflation like any imaginary ogre is mostly a façade, all one has to do is face it down and it will mostly go away on its own.

In fact deflation is nature's way of bringing sanity and rebirth to a society when it is rotting away with moral and other kinds of decay. The smartest thing this government can do is face reality and prepare for the inevitable. I know its bitter medicine but if we want to survive it must be taken. Practical all farm subsidies should be eliminated to force people to learn how and start planting because survival always at some point boils down to having enough food to eat.

When deflation comes and believe me it is coming, it is going to be like a fast moving wild fire. We will have very little time and one last chance to prevent going back to the Stone Age. The last chance would be to have mass tax cuts across the board that would produce the necessary fire break to stop runaway deflation from destroying everything.

The government should be prepared to cut off all spending except internal and external defense, departments of treasure, interior, and one or two others. Provide soup kitchens, home shelters, hospitals, and other bare necessities, everyone else are on their own. That is why the nuclear family system is so important. I know my kind of thinking is extreme, outrageous, and out of the question, but when it comes to survival, to me nothing is out of the question.

Let just pray that I'm off my rocker and forget you read this. God save America.

THE END

SEE MY WEBSITE AT: FLSIRMANS.COM